# 12 THINGS TO KNOW ABOUT
# THE MESOLITHIC ERA

by Meg Marquardt

STORY LIBRARY

MORE TO EXPLORE

www.12StoryLibrary.com

12-Story Library is an imprint of Bookstaves.

Photographs ©: PavleMarjanovic/Shutterstock.com, cover, 1; Oleg Senkov/Shutterstock.com, 4; Quizimodo/Polaris999/PD, 5; Esteban De Armas/Shutterstock.com, 5; Kim Christensen/Shutterstock.com, 6; José-Manuel Benito Álvarez/CC2.5, 6; The Portable Antiquities Scheme/The Trustees of the British Museum/CC2.0, 7; akg-images/Newscom, 8; Wolfgang Sauber/CC4.0, 9; PNAS/CC4.0, 10; PNAS/CC4.0, 11; mirjana ristic damjanovic/Shutterstock.com, 11; David Hawgood/CC2.0, 12; LundUniversity/YouTube, 13; Gary Todd/PD, 14; PNAS/CC4.0, 15; Nicolas Primola/Shutterstock.com, 16; W. Scott McGill/Shutterstock.com, 17; Athens and Macedonian News Agency, 18; Tolis-3kala/CC4.0, 19; PD, 20; garethwiscombe/CC2.0, 21; Henry Flower/CC3.0, 22; gerasimov_foto_174/Shutterstock.com, 23; Star Carr/YouTube, 24; CC3.0, 25; INTERFOTO/History/Alamy, 26; erichon/Shutterstock.com, 27; Gary Todd/PD, 29

**ISBN**
9781632357694 (hardcover)
9781632358783 (paperback)
9781645820505 (cbook)

**Library of Congress Control Number: 2019938629**

Printed in the United States of America
July 2019

About the Cover
Reconstruction of a world-famous Mesolithic house in Serbia.

Access free, up-to-date content on this topic plus a full digital version of this book. Scan the QR code on page 31 or use your school's login at 12StoryLibrary.com.

# Table of Contents

# 1 Change Happened at Different Times in Different Places

Glaciers began to retreat in the early part of the Mesolithic era.

The cold came out of nowhere. The world had been slowly warming. But 14,500 years ago, the cold came back with a snap. Glaciers started growing across Europe and North America. Sea levels fell. Those living in northern regions had to endure several thousand years of cold.

Then, 11,500 years ago, the cold suddenly reversed. Slowly, the world warmed again. The glaciers started to retreat. Sea levels started to rise. A brand-new period for humankind began.

The Mesolithic era is the middle part of the Stone Age. It is like a bridge. On one end of the bridge are Paleolithic people, the earliest humans. They are hunter-gatherers. On the other end of the bridge are Neolithic people. They are early farmers.

The Mesolithic era is everything and everyone in between. It lasts from around 10,000 years ago to 5,000 years ago. At the start, humans move around a lot to find food. By the end, they are beginning to grow

**8,000**
**Years ago when Doggerland was submerged**

- Doggerland was land exposed by low sea levels.
- It connected Britain to mainland Europe.
- When sea levels rose, Doggerland disappeared.

Doggerland as it is believed to have looked around 10,000 BCE.

crops and raise animals. In the middle, they get better at making tools. They develop bigger and more complex societies. And they change their approaches to art and building.

The Mesolithic era lasted for different amounts of time in different locations. That's because glaciers retreat at different speeds in different parts of the world. The Mesolithic era ended in southern Europe around 7,000 years ago. But it wouldn't end in northern Europe for another 3,000 years.

Early Mesolithic humans began to improve their hunting skills.

5

# Mesolithic People Made Better Tools

Humans aren't the only ones who use tools. But they are the best at making new tools. In the Mesolithic era, the big game-changer was using flints in new ways.

Flints are flaky bits of rock. Flint comes from a rock called quartz. Using other rocks, flint can be shaped. Flakes of stone will break away. This lets flints be formed into different types of tools.

Flint scrapers from the Mesolithic era.

For example, a flint could be made into a scraper. Scrapers have a sharp edge. They are like early knives, only made of rock instead of metal. Scrapers were used to clean, stretch, and soften animal hides. Hides are dried animal skins. Scrapers could turn them into clothing.

Microliths were other Mesolithic tools. They were small, very sharp flakes from a flint. They could be smaller than a finger. Microliths made good weapons. They could be attached to arrows and spears.

Microliths were small, but effective weapons.

# 4
## Length in inches (10 cm) of some large scrapers

- Most other scrapers were much smaller.
- Some were maybe too small to be used by an adult.
- Scrapers were also used to turn animal hides into tents.

To an untrained eye, Mesolithic tools might look like any other rocks. But archaeologists look for specific things. They might find a site full of microliths and microburins. Microburins are waste flakes left over from making microliths. Or they might find rocks that show signs of "working." Their edges are worn and chipped from shaping other tools.

Microburins, or waste flakes, are more uneven in shape.

## PREHISTORIC GLUE

Mesolithic people needed a way to attach sharp rocks to sticks. Then they could make weapons. So they figured out how to make tar. Tar can be made by slowly heating branches. As the branches heat up, they break down. They turn into a sticky substance that hardens over time. It is sticky enough to hold a piece of stone to an arrow or spear.

# Different Animals Meant New Ways to Hunt

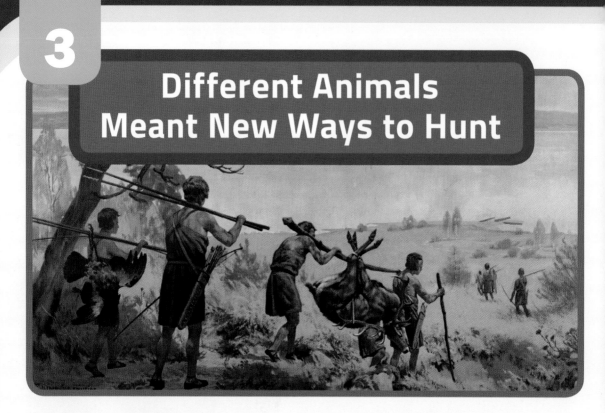

Humans adapted when temperatures changed from cold to warm. So did plants and animals. This meant that humans had to adjust their hunting techniques.

Before the Mesolithic era, hunters followed large animals that traveled in large herds. But after the ice melted, animals got smaller. They also moved in smaller herds. Before, a large group of hunters would have to work together to take down a big beast. But now, a smaller group or a single hunter could use arrows to kill animals like bison and reindeer.

There is evidence that some Mesolithic people fished for food. Researchers found a collection of fish bones in Croatia. The bones date from around the Mesolithic era. Researchers estimate that over

## 5
### Number of Stone Age bows found in Denmark

- The bows are 9,000 years old.
- They are the world's oldest bows.
- They were made of elm wood.

1,000 pounds (500 kg) of fish were caught and eaten. Other researchers have found early fishhooks. These were made of bone.

There is also some evidence that Mesolithic people started domesticating animals. All animals were once wild. Cows, sheep, and horses weren't always found on farms. By the end of the Mesolithic era, humans had domesticated at least pigs. Many farm animals were domesticated by the end of the Stone Age.

## HUMAN HEADS FOUND ON STAKES

Usually, the weapons archaeologists find are related to hunting. But a shocking discovery in 2009 showed that weapons were also used for other reasons. A construction project in Sweden uncovered Mesolithic remains. These included heads stuck on wooden stakes. Scientists aren't sure why the heads were impaled. Maybe they were put on display after the bodies were buried. Scientists are still trying to understand this mystery.

Mesolithic fishing hooks were made of animal bone.

# 4

# Mesolithic People Stayed Put

Ice cover stops a lot of plants from growing. When the ground is too cold, grasses can't grow thick and lush. Imagine wintertime, with snow covering everything. Now imagine winter lasting for thousands of years. Animals had to migrate to find enough food to live. If animals are moving, then humans who hunt them have to move, too.

But when the ice started to retreat and the grasses started to grow, animals were able to stick around in one area. That meant humans could do the same. They still had to move around a bit. After all, winters still came and went. But they could stay in the same general region. This stability allowed Mesolithic people to start building more permanent settlements.

One thing they built was storage houses. These could be used to store food and other things. Storage houses were

Storage houses had elevated floors to preserve and protect food.

Storage houses were encased with a thick coating of mud.

like outposts. A group could leave food behind and move on to a new location. During winter, when many animals had migrated away, the group could return to those food stores. They were also an important safety net in times when food got scarce.

## HOLOCENE VS. PLEISTOCENE

Scientists break up really big time periods into smaller chunks. Each chunk covers major events. The time period we are in now is called the Quaternary. It is split into smaller chunks called the Pleistocene and the Holocene. The Holocene starts when the last ice age ends. The Mesolithic era is the start of the Holocene. The Holocene is still going on today.

# 100
## Number of years at least one Mesolithic house was in use

- The house was found in Britain.
- Inside the house were several fireplaces built at different times.
- Researchers think the house was used for many generations.

# 5

# Many Mesolithic Societies Lived Along the Coasts

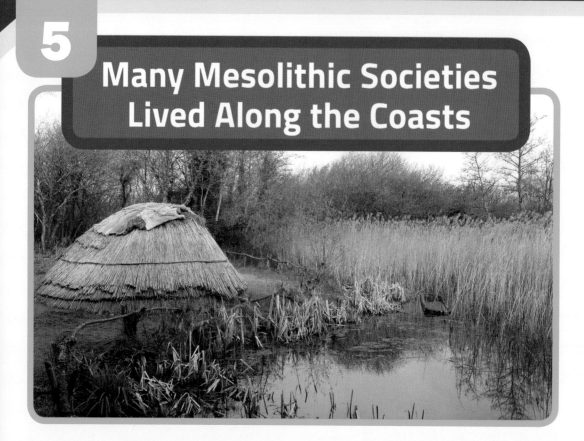

Just like people today, Mesolithic people liked living near water. But as the water rose, those settlements were covered. Today, many archaeological sites are underwater. To explore them, scientists use underwater archaeology techniques.

Underwater archaeology uses special tools. One is sonar. Sonar sends out sound waves underwater. Those sound waves bounce off objects. The sound waves come back to a detector. How long it takes the waves to travel tells the detector how far away the objects are. Sonar can tell if there is a strange object on the ocean floor.

One recent find was off the coast of Denmark. It is 6,000 years old. Researchers found over 60 arrowheads. They also found bones and wood that had been marked by Mesolithic tools. Because the artifacts were underwater, they were well preserved. The researchers even found a piece of amber that might have been part of a large necklace.

# 65

**Depth underwater in feet (20 m) of one Mesolithic city**

- The city is off the coast of Sweden.
- Scientists have found remains of a fishing settlement, including 9,000-year-old fish traps.
- They also found a 9,000-year-old hand axe made of elk antler.

## THINK ABOUT IT

If you could look for ancient civilizations off the coast of any country, where would you look? Why?

Archaeologists are looking in the North Sea, off the coast of the United Kingdom. They know that area wouldn't have been underwater 10,000 years ago. They think it is likely large groups of people once lived in the region. But this is a challenge of underwater archaeology. The researchers have to use educated guesses about where to look. They mapped the area with sonar. They think a huge lake once existed there. They are looking on the banks of that lake. Perhaps their educated guesses will turn up evidence of Mesolithic people.

The 9,000 year-old axe was found underwater off the coast of Sweden in 2016.

# Mesolithic People Probably Did Not Farm

People who study the Mesolithic era debate a lot about farming. Farming is a big deal. People who can farm are more advanced. Researchers use different methods to try and figure out who farmed and who did not.

One thing researchers look at is ancient pollen. Pollen is like a fine dust that forms inside of seed plants. When pollen is released, it eventually falls to the ground. That pollen can be trapped under layers of dirt. If archaeologists know how old the dirt is, they know how old the pollen is.

Each plant gives off its own type of pollen. Researchers can look for a specific pollen to know what kind of plants grew in that area. In some Mesolithic settlements, there is evidence of domesticated grain. This is grain that was planted and raised as crops, not just found and eaten. Researchers think these Mesolithic people may have been growing plants.

But just because they were eating the grains doesn't mean they were

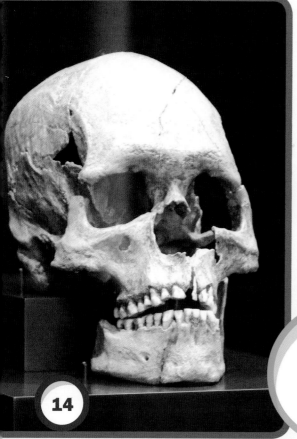

Skull with teeth from 7500 BCE.

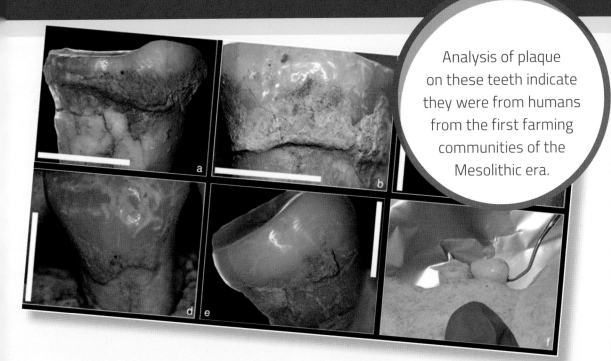

Analysis of plaque on these teeth indicate they were from humans from the first farming communities of the Mesolithic era.

farming. These Mesolithic people might have come into contact with a more advanced civilization. That civilization may have shared their domesticated grains with the Mesolithic people. Because civilizations were mixing, it might never be clear exactly how much Mesolithic people took part in agriculture.

# 9
## Mesolithic people whose teeth provided important clues

- Researchers found nine sets of human remains in Serbia.
- They studied the 8,000-year-old plaque on their teeth.
- Tiny fossilized bits of domesticated plants were trapped in the plaque.

## NUT ROAST

Mesolithic people also ate a lot of nuts. At a house built over 10,000 years ago, researchers found burnt hazelnut shells. Since they were burnt, scientists thought they had been roasted over a fire. Nuts were an important part of a hunter-gatherer diet.

# Life in the Americas Was Different

When glaciers trapped a bunch of water, it was enough to create a land bridge between Asia and North America. Early humans walked across that land bridge. But when the ice retreated, the ocean flooded back in. The Old World was cut off from the New World.

The Old World is Europe, Asia, and Africa. Their ancient history is split between three time periods. Mesolithic is the middle time period. The New World is the Americas. There isn't complete consensus about how to divide ancient history

for the early Americans. Some archaeologists split it into five different periods. Others split it into six. No matter how you cut it, early Americans were facing the same challenges as Mesolithic people in the Old World.

The time when humans first appeared in the Americas is called the Paleoindian Period. Some also call it the Lithic Stage. That's because these New World people were working with lithic tools, just like people in the Old World. Lithic tools are tools made of stone. During this period, people migrated

# Around 1000

### Year of first contact between the Old World and the New World

- Viking explorer Leif Eriksson was born in Greenland.
- He is believed to be the first European to set foot in North America.
- This was 500 years before Christopher Columbus.

## THINK ABOUT IT

If you could live in the Old World or the New World, which would you choose? Why?

These people were great hunters. They took down large game, like bison. They created different types of spear points, depending on where they lived. For example, the southeastern United States was known as the Dalton region. Dalton arrows were leaf-shaped and serrated. They were also sharpened over and over. This shows that Dalton had excellent stoneworkers.

down from what would become Canada to settle the Great Plains and a bit further south.

Dalton arrowheads dating from 8,000 to 9,000 years ago.

# Mesolithic People May Have Looked More Masculine

Mesolithic people had a lot in common with modern-day humans. They lived in groups. They ate some of the same food we eat today. They created art and jewelry. But they probably didn't look quite like we do.

We know how they might have looked. Some scientists specialize in facial reconstruction. They can look at ancient bones and re-create what a person might have looked like. Reconstruction requires a lot of knowledge from different fields. You need to know how bones fit together. You need to understand how muscles fit over bones. You have to understand how the environment can change how someone looks. For example, someone living in Africa will have darker skin. Finally, you need the artistic skill to bring it all together.

Often, teams of scientists work together. That happened with the remains of a young woman who lived 9,000 years ago. Scientists scanned her skull to create a three-dimensional model. Then they made clay shaped like muscles. Once the muscles were in place, they put on more clay for her skin. The team guessed at what she might look like. Since the bones were found in Greece, they gave her dark hair and dark eyes.

The reconstructed face of Avgi.

The cave where Avgi's bones were excavated.

In the end, they had the face of a young woman with a protruding jaw and dimpled chin. Her eyes are set close together. She has prominent cheekbones and a heavy brow. These are usually considered more masculine features. Looking at her teeth, the scientists guessed she was 18 years old when she died. They named her Avgi. In Greek, Avgi means "dawn."

# 1993

**Year when Avgi's bones were found in Thessaly, Greece**

- They were found in a cave. They had never been disturbed.
- Archaeologists had been excavating the cave for seven years.
- These were the first bones of a Mesolithic human found in Thessaly.

# Mesolithic People May Have Practiced Ritual Sacrifice

A new hunting season is about to start. Leaders of a Mesolithic band capture a young deer. They drown the deer in a lake. This is a sacrifice to the god of the hunt. It's believed this sacrifice will bring a year of good hunting.

It's not possible to know if this is exactly what happened. There isn't any writing that tells us what ancient people believed. But archaeologists have ways to make educated guesses.

One way is to look at cultures that still practice ancient ways. An example is the Nenet tribe in Siberia. The Nenets are reindeer herders. Researchers think they have maintained some of their cultural ways for 10,000 years. The Nenets practice reindeer sacrifice. By looking at this living example,

researchers can guess what ancient cultures might have done.

Researchers can also make guesses based on archaeological finds. One of the most famous ancient monuments is Stonehenge. Stonehenge is in Britain. It is a collection of huge stone pillars and arches. Mesolithic people didn't build Stonehenge. However, there have been discoveries near Stonehenge that date to the Mesolithic era.

Stonehenge dates from many time periods.

# 35,000+
**Pieces of worked flint found at Blick Mead**

- Blick Mead is about 1.5 miles (2.4 km) from Stonehenge.
- The flint pieces date from Mesolithic times.
- Archaeologists believe large Mesolithic feasts and gatherings once took place there.

## STONEHENGE

Stonehenge is a complicated site. There are ruins from Mesolithic times. There are also ruins from at least three other time periods. By the time the main monument was built, a lot of different cultures had added to the site. Stonehenge is an example of how a site can persist through time and last through different cultures.

# Mesolithic Artists Drew Other Humans

People who lived before the Mesolithic era were concerned with drawing animals. Mesolithic people didn't stop drawing animals. They just added a new character. Mesolithic artists were really interested in drawing humans.

Mesolithic people also changed where they made their drawings. Art used to be mostly on cave walls. Now art starts showing up outdoors, in the open.

Drawings of people hunting are found all over cliffs and stone outcroppings. This could be because it was warmer, and people could spend more time outdoors. But why they chose a particular stone cliff over another isn't clear.

Mesolithic artists were good at capturing movement. Rock paintings show people dancing or hunting. Artists captured movement in a couple of ways. Sometimes, it was

# 10,000
## Age in years of the oldest known crayon

- The crayon was found in Britain. It is made of red ochre, a type of clay.
- It shows a wear pattern similar to a modern-day pencil or crayon.
- It was likely used to make rock drawings.

the dancers tilted, it looks like they are having a party.

Archaeologists are particularly interested in the way Mesolithic artists drew human figures. Mesolithic art is considered highly stylized. This means the artist didn't try to show the object as it looked in real life. Think about a cartoon dog with huge eyes and a big head. It doesn't look like a real dog. It's stylized.

Mesolithic human drawings are stick figures. Archaeologists think they might be pictographs. Pictographs are a very early form of writing. Mesolithic people might have been using drawing as a way of writing.

obvious, like drawing legs that look like they are running. Other times, it was more subtle. Artists slightly tilted human figures. Imagine a drawing of a dancer. She has her hands up in the air. She is tilted away from other dancers. With all

23

# 11

## Mesolithic People Created Jewelry and Carvings

It's believed the Star Carr pendant was worn for spiritual protection.

Most Mesolithic jewelry makers lived in Scandinavia. They made pendants. These pendants were made of stone with a hole in the corner. A piece of fiber could be run through the hole to make a necklace.

One of the most famous Mesolithic pendants is the Star Carr pendant. It's famous because of where it was found. It wasn't found in Scandinavia. It was found in Britain. It is made of shale and has a crosshatch line pattern. This same pattern is found on a lot of pendants from Denmark. Researchers aren't sure how the Star Carr ended up in Britain. Maybe someone migrated from Denmark. Or maybe a British artist heard about this style of jewelry and tried to make one. How it came to Britain will probably always be a mystery.

Mesolithic artists also made relief carvings. In this type of carving, the wood or stone around an object is

# THE SHIGIR IDOL

The Shigir Idol is one of the most striking pieces of Mesolithic art. It is the oldest wooden statue in the world. It was shaped to look like a man. It is over 16 feet (5 m) tall. The sculpture was found in Russia. Researchers think that beaver teeth were used to make the intricate carvings in the wood.

carved away. The object seems to be jumping out of the background. Famous Mesolithic reliefs are found at Göbeckli Tepe in Turkey. This is a very important archaeological site. Stone walls and pillars are covered with relief carvings. There are ducks, snakes, and foxes. Also scorpions, bulls, and vultures.

The Shigir Idol is on display at the Sverdlovsk Regional Local Lore Museum in Russia.

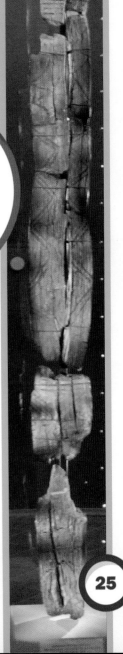

# 39

**Length in feet (12 m) of a Mesolithic monolith found in the Mediterranean**

- The monolith is 131 feet (40 m) underwater.
- It could be up to 10,000 years old. It might have been a monument.
- The people who made it must have had technical and engineering skills.

# The Rise of Farming Drove Out Mesolithic Cultures

The Mesolithic way of life died out because something better came along. Mesolithic people were great at making tools to take down game. They could forage for nuts and vegetables. They built some lasting structures. Even though they were nomadic, they stuck around the same general area.

But warm weather meant two events were happening at once. First, glaciers were retreating and sea levels were rising. Mesolithic cultures living on the edge of the sea would have faced water creeping onto their land. They would have had to move farther inland, abandoning what they had built.

Second, other people were on the move. These new people had an important new skill. They knew how

# 100
## Estimated number of uncontacted tribes around the world

- Uncontacted tribes do not interact with the outside world.
- They have lived the same way for thousands of years.
- Countries create laws to stop people from making contact with these tribes.

to farm. While Mesolithic peoples were still hunting and gathering, these new people could live in one spot. They could build bigger settlements and grow populations.

The end of the Mesolithic era is marked by the rise of farming. As soon as farmers moved in, ways of life changed. Mesolithic people could not keep up with these new technologies. Farming took over everything.

Hunter-gatherer societies didn't totally disappear. Though the Mesolithic era ended 8,000 years ago, there are still hunter-gatherer groups today. They are mostly located in Africa, South America, and on remote islands. They use bows and arrows to hunt. Most do not use a lot of modern technology. These groups and their ways of life are protected. Some part of the Mesolithic way of life still exists today.

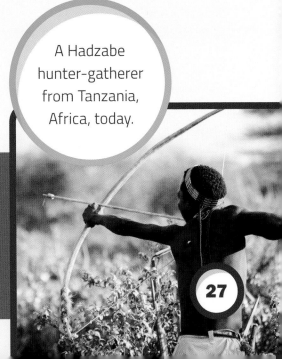

A Hadzabe hunter-gatherer from Tanzania, Africa, today.

## THINK ABOUT IT

If you could live like a hunter-gatherer, what job would you like? Would you be a hunter or a gatherer? Or would you be an artist?

# Timeline of the Mesolithic Era

**The Mesolithic Era—the Middle Stone Age—lasted from 10,000 years ago to 5,000 years ago.**

**10,000 years ago:**
The last ice age ends.

**10,000 years ago:**
Rock art shows evidence of some of the earliest recorded warfare.

**9,500 years ago:**
Mesolithic people are making sharp tools for hunting.

**8,600 years ago:**
Mesolithic people are gathering at Blick Mead near Stonehenge.

**8,000 years ago:**
Rising sea levels cut Britain off from the mainland.

**7,000 years ago:**
Fishing villages are bringing in huge hauls of fish.

**6,600 years ago:**
People are eating domesticated grain.

**5,000 years ago:**
Farming societies start to take over the Mesolithic era.

A mortar and pestle from the Mesolithic era.

# Glossary

**adapt**
To change in response to environmental changes.

**concensus**
Agreement among all the people in a group.

**domesticate**
To turn wild animals into tamer ones; to grow a plant for human use.

**glacier**
Large, slow-moving sheet of ice.

**herder**
Someone who takes care of animals.

**impale**
To stick a spear or a stick through something.

**migrate**
To move from one place to another.

**monolith**
A tall, straight pillar.

**plaque**
A buildup on teeth.

**quartz**
A white, brown, or clear flaky stone.

**remains**
The dead body of a person or animal; parts of something that are left when the rest is gone.

**serrated**
A jagged edge.

**submerge**
To cover with water or another liquid.

# Read More

Felix, Rebecca. *Unearthing Early Human Remains*. Minneapolis, MN: ABDO Publishing, 2019.

Ganeri, Anita. *Writing History: Stone Age*. London, UK: Franklin Watts, 2019.

Mooney, Carla. *Evolution: How Life Adapts to a Changing Environment*. River Junction, VT: Nomad Press, 2017.

## Visit 12StoryLibrary.com

Scan the code or use your school's login at **12StoryLibrary.com** for recent updates about this topic and a full digital version of this book. Enjoy free access to:

- Digital ebook
- Breaking news updates
- Live content feeds
- Videos, interactive maps, and graphics
- Additional web resources

**Note to educators:** Visit 12StoryLibrary.com/register to sign up for free premium website access. Enjoy live content plus a full digital version of every 12-Story Library book you own for every student at your school.

# Index

## About the Author

Meg Marquardt started out as a scientist but likes writing about science even more. She enjoys researching physics, geology, and climate science. She lives in Madison, Wisconsin, with her two scientist cats, Lagrange and Doppler.

32